Stress Relief for Kids
Taming Your Dragons

Stress Relief for Kids
Taming Your Dragons

by

Martha Belknap

Whole Person Associates
Duluth, Minnesota

Whole Person Associates
210 West Michigan
Duluth, MN 55802
1-800-247-6789

Stress Relief for Kids
Taming Your Dragons

Illustrations by: Ray Kemble, Denise Harris Kester, and Kristen
Baumgardner Caven

Printed in the United States of America.

Library of Congress Control Number: 2005938637

ISBN 978-1-57025-242-6

Dedication

With thanks to the many children in my classes
who have helped me learn the importance of
taming my dragons

Table of Contents

Poems and Songs

Greetings from the Author

When *Taming Your Dragons* was first published in 1986, I had no idea how far my dragons would help me fly. My second book, *Taming More Dragons*, was released in 1994 and was the continuation of a creative process that is still going on.

Currently I share my dragon activities with the preschool children in my music classes at two Montessori schools. I teach the same ideas to Mexican women in my English as a Second Language classes. I include similar principles in my training workshops for prospective yoga instructors. Some of my most receptive students are the beautiful seniors in my yoga classes for the elderly. What started out as a collection of creative relaxation activities for children has expanded into a repertoire of experiences for anyone who is young at heart.

Since I began playing around with dragons, I have moved from the mountains near Boulder, Colorado, to Cardiff, a town on the coast of southern California. I went from elementary special education to university teaching, and then from retirement to three part-time jobs. Along the way I have balanced my passion for skiing with my love for boogie boarding.

I am delighted that my first two books are now republished in one volume along with some recent additions. I hope you will enjoy learning and teaching these activities and adding your original inspirations and innovations to them. Strive to maintain a healthy balance of energies on the mental, physical, emotional, and spiritual levels. Above all, have fun taming your dragons.

I give loving thanks to my husband, Bill Brennen, for continuing to encourage my creativity and to the many students from 3 to 93 who have inspired me to expand and grow.

Using This Book

The following activities are designed to be read aloud very slowly and clearly. Use a calm, quiet voice and pause a few seconds at the end of each sentence. Your listeners will need plenty of time to enjoy every step of the experience without feeling hurried.

Be sure to end each activity with some gentle suggestions such as, "Begin to stretch like a cat; open your eyes very slowly; come back to a sitting position when you feel ready." For the guided imagery activities I recommend a warm, carpeted area and low lights.

I suggest doing all these activities yourself before trying them with others.

These directions serve only as a guide for the reader. You may want to change the wording or the length of the activity. Use your creativity to expand these images as you wish.

You may want to tape record the directions and/or play quiet music in the background.

Many of these activities can lead very naturally into creative writing and art experiences. Encourage group discussions and sharing of feelings afterwards.

Help children learn to direct themselves and each other in these activities.

I sincerely hope that you will enjoy participating in these creative relaxation experiences.

Centering

I Am Relaxed

Purpose: feel quiet inside

Sit comfortably and close your eyes.
Let go of your face.
Feel your mouth and chin relax.
Listen to your quiet breathing.
As you breathe in, say to yourself, "I am."
As you breathe out, say to yourself, "relaxed."
Continue to breathe gently and easily.
Continue to say, "I am... relaxed."
Continue to listen to your quiet breathing.
After a while you may want to change the words to:
"I am calm." "I am peaceful." "I am quiet."
Let yourself find the words and feelings which are best for you.
Feel your quiet, peaceful place inside.

Let's Look Inside

Purpose: feel warm and peaceful inside

Sit comfortably and close your eyes.

Say these words to yourself:

(as you breathe in)	(as you breathe out)
I close my eyes...	and look inside my head
I listen to my breathing...	and quiet my thoughts
I let my body be still...	and relax my face
I feel my heartbeat...	and let go of tightness
I feel into my center...	and feel warm inside
I see a rainbow in the sky...	and am filled with peace

Let peaceful thoughts come to your mind.

Light Up The Dark

Purpose: feel light inside

Sit comfortably and close your eyes.
Look into the darkness behind your eyes.
Imagine the space inside your head.
Breathe light into that darkness.
See light in the center of your head.
Imagine the space inside your chest.
Breathe light into that darkness.
See light in the center of your chest.
Imagine the space inside your belly.
Breathe light into that darkness.
See light in the center of your belly.
Now find the space inside that you like the best.
Breathe warm air into that space.
See light inside of you.
Pretend you are inside that center space.
Enjoy being quiet there.

Down the Stairs

Purpose: feel centered

Sit comfortably and close your eyes.

Listen to your breathing.

Imagine that you are standing at the top of a long stairway.

Breathe in and picture the number 10.

As you breathe out, take one step down and picture the number 9.

Breathe in again.

As you breathe out, take one step down and picture the number 8.

Breathe in again.

Each time you breathe out, take another step down and continue to count backwards.

When you reach number 1, imagine that you are at the bottom of the stairs.

You are standing in a beautiful garden.

Notice what is growing there.

Notice the wonderful smells.

Notice all the different colors. Listen to the sounds.

Begin to walk around very slowly.

Continue to breathe quietly as you enjoy everything that you see and hear and smell in the garden.

A Shining Star

Purpose: feel strong and rested

Sit comfortably and close your eyes.

Imagine the dark sky at night.

Look up at the bright stars.

See the word STAR in your mind.

Imagine the letters S-T-A-R on the inside of your eyelids.

As you look at the letter S, breathe in strength.

Feel strength inside your body.

As you look at the letter T, breathe in trust.

Feel trust inside your heart.

As you look at the letter A, breathe in awareness.

Feel awareness inside your mind.

As you look at the letter R, breathe in rest.

Feel rest inside your whole self.

Now picture a beautiful, bright shining star.

Feel the peace of the night sky.

Let your own star be very special for you.

See how brightly it shines.

Stretching

Crazy Mixed-Up Umbrella

Purpose: stretch your chest and upper back

Stand with your feet comfortably apart.
Clasp your hands together behind your seat.
Breathe in as you tilt your head back a little.
Breathe out as you lean forward from the hips.
Lift your arms up over your back, hands still clasped.
Bend forward as your neck and head relax.
Press your elbows toward each other.
Imagine an umbrella turned inside out.
Now the wind is blowing a little harder.
Continue to breathe easily as you stretch and hold.
Breathe in and lift up slowly to a standing position.
Relax your arms and rest.
Shake all the rain out of your umbrella.

Become Your Favorite Cat

Purpose: stretch your chest and middle back

Kneel down on all fours like a cat.

Breathe in slowly through your nose.

As you breathe out, bring your right knee toward your nose.

Feel the curl in your back as you hold the stretch.

Breathe in and lift your right leg in the air behind you.

Lift your head and look up.

Feel the arch in your back as you hold the stretch.

Breathe out and return to all fours.

Rest and notice how you feel.

Repeat the stretch with your left leg.

Breathe out and return to all fours.

Now meow like your favorite cat!

Monster Mask

Purpose: stretch and relax your face

Sit comfortably and close your eyes.

Imagine a very ugly monster.

Pretend to put on a monster mask.

Squeeze everything in your face toward the end of your nose.

Wiggle your mouth and chin from side to side.

Make some wrinkles in your forehead and around your eyes.

Open your mouth wide and stick out your tongue.

Make an ugly monster sound.

Now take off your monster mask.

Let all the muscles in your face go limp.

Relax your eyes, your cheeks, and your jaw.

Rest your whole face.

Repeat this stretch several times.

Then enjoy complete relaxation in your face.

Now quietly say "Good-bye" to the monster.

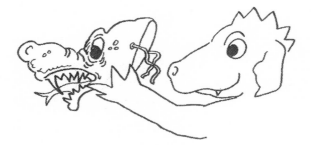

Picking Peaches

Purpose: stretch your whole body

Stand with your feet comfortably apart.

Pretend you are in a beautiful orchard.

In front of you is your favorite fruit tree.

Reach up with one arm over your head.

Let the opposite heel lift off the ground.

Pretend you are picking a peach... or a pear... or a plum... or whatever fruit you like best.

Now lift up the other arm and the other heel.

Continue to pick fruit as you stretch from one side to the other.

Gather as many pieces of fruit as you wish.

Pretend to take a bite of one.

Taste how sweet and juicy it is.

Offer to share your fruit with a friend.

Say, "I'd like a bite of your apple. Would you like an apricot?"

Pick some more fruit and share another bite with someone else.

Trees in the Breeze

Purpose: stretch your whole body

Stand with your feet comfortably apart.

Breathe in and lift your arms overhead.

Link your thumbs together.

Imagine a palm tree on the beach in Hawaii.

Sway from side to side in the breeze.

(long pause)

Think about an oak tree in the summertime.

Stretch your leafy branches out and down to the side of your trunk.

(long pause)

Pretend you are a willow tree.

Bend your trunk and branches forward over the lazy river in front of you.

(long pause)

Stand up and imagine an apple tree in the fall. Feel your branches heavy with fruit.

Some children come by and shake you so your apples fall to the ground.

Let them shake you a little harder.

(long pause)

Imagine a pine tree in the forest.

Stretch your tall straight trunk up toward the sun.

Send your long roots deep down into the earth.

 (long pause)

Pretend you are a beautiful Christmas tree being decorated.

Wrap shiny silver tinsel all around your branches.

(long pause)

What other trees can you think of?

How can you move like one of them?

Seaweed, Sunflower, and Oak

Purpose: become aware of different energy levels

Note: Read very slowly

Stand with your arms relaxed at your sides, knees bent slightly, and eyes closed.

Slowly let your weight shift easily from side to side.

Picture a piece of seaweed firmly attached to the ocean floor, yet free to move gently with the changing tide.

Focus your attention above your head and imagine becoming that piece of seaweed.

You are drifting, floating, shifting with the current, feeling light and relaxed.

Notice how freely you move.

Come back to center and open your eyes.

Now close your eyes again.

Picture a tall yellow sunflower growing at the edge of a garden.

Focus your attention into your chest and imagine becoming that sunflower.

Take in a breath and then exhale as your head rolls forward.

As you breathe in again, feel the flower waking up in the morning.

Slowly lift your head and look toward the sun.

Feel the warmth of the sun shining down on the muscles of your face.

Now breathe out as you lower your head toward your chest just as a sunflower bows to the earth at the end of the day.

Continue this movement a few more times.

Notice how flexible you are while still remaining strong.

Come back to center and open your eyes.

Now close your eyes again.

Picture a sturdy oak tree in the forest with firm roots growing down deep into the earth.

Focus your attention into your abdomen and imagine becoming that oak tree.

Be aware of the trunk of the tree and feel the roots growing out through the bottom of your feet into the ground.

Feel a strong connection with the earth beneath you.

Although the wind may blow through your branches, you are very safe, even in a storm.

You are grounded and centered, strong and relaxed.

Notice how powerful you are.

Come back to center and open your eyes.

Think about these three experiences.

Which one did you like the best?

Did you enjoy the freedom of the seaweed?

Were you aware of the flexibility of the sunflower?

Could you feel the power of the oak tree?

Are you more like one of these plants than another?

Are you like all three?

Are you able to change your energy from one to another when you want to?

Think also about the tumbleweed, which is weak and fragile, and the cactus, which is rigid and harsh.

What happens when two people with cactus type energy come together?

Or when two tumbleweed people try to make decisions?

As you remember the seaweed, the sunflower, and the oak tree, keep yourself balanced with freedom, flexibility, and power.

Imagine You're a Dragon

Purpose: stretch your body in seven different ways

Stand comfortably with your arms relaxed at your side.
Let go of the tightness in your knees.
Imagine you're a dragon who lives up North.
You like cold weather and snowstorms.
Breathe in and lift your arms up over your head.
Move your arms like the cold winds of the north.
Let the snow fly during a big blizzard.
Lower your arms and relax.

Imagine you're a dragon who lives along the East coast.
You like to play in the ocean.
Breathe in and lift your arms up to waist level.
Move your arms around your body like giant waves.
Let the waves roll in along the shore.
Lower your arms and relax.
Imagine you're a dragon who lives in the South.
You like warm weather and sunshine.
Breathe in and lift your arms to the side with your palms facing up.
Feel the sun rise over your head.
Lower your hands down over your face and body.
Feel the sun showering you with its warm energy.

Imagine you're a dragon who lives along the California coast or in Hawaii.

You like palm trees and tropical weather.

Breathe in and lift your arms up over your head.

Move like a palm tree swaying in the breeze.

Feel the stretch in your trunk and limbs.

Lower your branches and let go.

Imagine you're a dragon who lives in the Midwest

You like wide open fields of wheat and corn.

Breathe in and lift your arms up to shoulder level.

Stretch your fingers out as far as you can in every direction.

Reach out over acres and acres of farmland.

Lower your arms and relax.

Imagine you're a dragon who lives in the Rocky Mountains

You like snowy peaks and high elevations.

Breathe in and lift your arms up as high as you can.

Climb up to the Continental Divide.

Reach up to the top of the highest mountain and look out at the view! Go down to the bottom of the mountain and relax.

Imagine you're a dragon who lives in the Southwest desert.

You like open skies and beautiful sunsets.

Breathe in and lift your arms up all around you.

Feel the openness of the sky filled with giant clouds.

Stretch your whole body out into space.

Now let go and relax completely.

Drakely the Dragon Says

Purpose: This activity may be played like "Simon Says" or simply used as a stretching and relaxation exercise.

Drakely the Dragon says...

open your eyes wide like an owl

close your eyes like a newborn kitten

lift your eyebrows up toward your hair

pull up on your donkey ears

wiggle your nose like a bunny

blow up your cheeks like a chipmunk

grin like the Cheshire cat

show your teeth like an angry wolf

open your mouth like a roaring dragon and roar

scrunch up your face like a wrinkled prune

move your lips like a kissing fish

stick out your tongue like a frog catching flies

stick out your chin like a monkey

pull your head into your shoulders like a turtle in a shell

stretch out your neck like a giraffe

puff up your chest like a gorilla

pound on your chest like Tarzan...
   and make some jungle sounds

spread your fingers apart like starfish

squeeze lemons in your fists and then drop them

close your eyes and let them roll up toward the top of
   your head like marbles

A Trip Through the Solar System

Purpose: stretch your body and release tension

Stand comfortably with your feet slightly apart.

Imagine that you are taking a trip through the solar system.

The first planet that you come to is Mercury, which travels very fast.

Shake your whole body, arms and legs, as fast as you can.

The next planet is Venus, which is surrounded by beautiful clouds.

Let your arms circle freely around your body and float easily above your head.

And now to planet Earth where you find plants and trees.

As you breathe in, draw your hands upwards through your trunk and stretch your branches out toward the sky.

On Mars there are polar ice caps.

Reach your arms overhead toward the North Pole.

Then bring them down as you reach forward toward the South Pole.

Beyond Mars there are asteroids flying around at very high speeds.

Make fists with both hands and pound on your chest.

Jupiter is the largest planet on your journey.

Extend your arms out around your body, becoming as heavy and powerful as possible.

Saturn is surrounded by rings.

Swing your arms around your waist, encircling your body.

Uranus has five moons in its orbit.

Flick your fingers outwards five times in different directions.

Then do it again.

Neptune was named after the mythical ruler of the sea.

Let your arms become like ocean waves that rise and fall all around your body.

Pluto is the farthest planet away from the sun, and it is extremely cold.

Shake and shiver your whole body as you feel how freezing it is out there.

Now imagine standing back on the earth, feeling the warmth of the sun shining down on your whole body.

Let the sun shower you with its rays of warmth and comfort.

Close your eyes and relax completely.

What's Your Phone Number?

Purpose: stretch your body and your memory

Stand comfortably with your feet slightly apart and your legs relaxed.

0   With your arms outstretched, trace a big 0 around your body. Imagine that you are playing with a hula hoop around your waist.

1   Reach both arms overhead. Trace a 1 in the air as you stretch a huge elastic band down to the ground.

2   Put your hands on your shoulders. Flap 2 wings in the air, up and down, forward and backward.

3   Do a 3-step cha-cha-cha as you snap your fingers or clap your hands. Shift your weight from side to side as you count 1 - 2 - 3 - rest.

4   Do a 4-step march as you raise your knees in front of your chest. Move your arms in rhythm as you count 1 - 2 - 3 - 4.

5   Shake 5 fingers of one hand, then 5 fingers of the other hand. Now shake one foot, and then the other foot. Now shake both hands and both feet all at once.

6   Make fists with your hands and climb 6 steps up
     the staircase on your back. Then run down and up
     again a few more times.

7   With your fists, pound on your chest like Tarzan
     as you say:
     1 - 2 - 3 - 4 - 5 - 6 - 7
     Makes me feel like I'm in heaven!

8   Imagine a figure 8 on the ground around your
     feet. Trace the 8 with your knees, your hips, and
     your shoulders.

9   Tap your seat with one hand and then the other
     as you say:
     1 - 2 - 3 - 4 - 5 - 6 - 7 - 8 - 9
     Moving makes my body feel so fine.

Stand and face another person.

Indicate your phone number by making the movements that go with each digit.

Ask your partner to figure out what your phone number is.

Tilt-a-Dragon

Purpose: stretch your body as you move together with three other people

In a group of four, sit on the floor with your feet in the middle of the circle.

Face toward the person opposite you.

Bend your knees and scoot forward until you can hold hands in a circle.

Number yourselves 1 - 2 - 3 - 4.

Numbers 1 and 3 lie down on your backs.

You may need to bend your knees a little more.

As numbers 2 and 4 begin to lie down, numbers 1 and 3 begin to sit up.

As numbers 1 and 3 begin to lie down, numbers 2 and 4 begin to sit up.

Continue moving up and down, establishing a rhythm for yourselves.

When your energy is coordinated, move a little faster.

Feel a good stretch in your stomach and lower back.

This activity is fun to do with two adults and two children.

Sit opposite the person who is closest to your size.

Breathing

Rainbow Clouds

Purpose: quiet your breathing

Lie down comfortably and close your eyes.

Imagine a clear blue summer sky overhead.

Notice some soft white fluffy clouds drifting by.

Invite one of those clouds to come visit you.

Watch it float down close to the ground.

Hide yourself inside of it.

Feel the cloud wrapped all around you.

Breathe in the softness of the cloud.

Watch the cloud become pink.

Breathe pink all around inside of you.

Notice how you are feeling.

Change the cloud to another color you like very much.

Breathe in your new color.

Notice how you are feeling now.

Change the color again... and again.

Breathe in all the colors you like the best.

(long pause)

Enjoy being wrapped in your rainbow.

Enjoy hiding inside your rainbow cloud.

What's for Dinner?

Purpose: develop sense of smell

Lie down comfortably and close your eyes.
Pretend you are curled up on a big soft pillow.
You are resting on your living room floor.
You begin to smell something wonderful.
Take a deep breath and smell it some more.
The smell is coming from the kitchen.
Breathe in and smell it again.
It is something you like very much.
Breathe in once more.
You smell something you'd like for dinner.
Notice if it is on the stove or in the oven.
Continue to breathe deeply and fully.
Take some time to enjoy the wonderful smell.
(long pause)
Open your eyes slowly and sit up.
Tell someone what you'd like for
dinner tonight.

The Alphabet Breath

Purpose: pay attention to what you need

Think about the initials of your name or any three letters you like.

Let each letter stand for an important quality in your life.

(If your letters are F.P.H., you could think of Fun, Patience, and Health.)

Sit comfortably and close your eyes.

Notice the darkness behind your eyelids.

Imagine the darkness of midnight and feel that darkness all around you.

In the far distance, picture a spot of bright light coming toward you.

As the light gets closer, notice what color it is.

Watch it form the first letter you have chosen.

Continue to trace the pattern of that letter in your imagination.

Remember the word that letter stands for.

Listen to the sound of that word inside your head.

Imagine breathing that quality into your mind.

Think about the importance of that word in your life.

Now imagine the first letter of that word moving off to the side.

Watch another spot of light coming toward you in the darkness.

As the light gets closer, it forms the second letter you have chosen.

(Continue this exercise with all three letters using the same directions.)

Repeat the three words to yourself slowly as you breathe in and out.

Five Breath Vacation

Purpose: quiet relaxation between activities

Sit comfortably and close your eyes.

Be aware of your breathing.

Listen to the sound of your breath.

Feel the air flowing gently in and out.

On your next breath, imagine a beautiful place you'd like to visit.

As you breathe out, feel yourself traveling there.

On your second breath in, notice the colors of your favorite place.

As you breathe out, enjoy the scene in every possible way.

On your third breath in, listen to the natural sounds of this place.

As you breathe out, be aware of the quietness you feel inside yourself.

On your fourth breath in, notice all the beauty surrounding you.

As you breathe out, relax into full enjoyment of this time and place.

On your fifth breath in, feel yourself traveling home again.

As you breathe out, stretch your arms and open your eyes.

Tell someone about your wonderful five breath vacation.

Belly Balloon

Purpose: let go of tightness.

Lie down comfortably and close your eyes.

Place one hand gently on your belly.

Breathe into your belly and feel your hand move up and down.

Imagine a balloon inside your belly.

As you breathe in, blow up the balloon. (long pause)

As you breathe out, empty the balloon. (long pause)
Blow up the balloon again.

Let the air leak out through your teeth with a long slow hissing sound.

Blow up the balloon again.

Imagine sticking a pin into the balloon.

Let the air escape through your mouth with a sudden POP!

Notice how relaxed you are.

Notice how good you feel inside.

Now picture the whole sky full of beautiful colored balloons.

Treasure Breathing

Purpose: feel relaxed and centered within

Sit quietly and close your eyes.

Listen to the sound of your breath.

Feel the gentle movement of your breath as you inhale and exhale.

On one line of the following poem, let your breath flow into your body.

On the next line of the poem, let your breath flow out of your body.

Poem: I let my precious treasures grow (inhale)
    As I let all my dragons go (exhale)

    I breathe in health and feel it flow
    As I let all diseases go

    I breathe in love and feel it flow
    As I let fear and anger go

    I breathe in joy and feel it flow
    As I let all my sadness go

    I breathe in strength and feel it flow
    As I let all my weakness go

    I breathe in warmth and feel it flow
    As I let all discomfort go

    I breathe in courage, feel it flow
    As I let cares and worries go

    I breathe in peace and feel it flow
    I'm filled with peace and I let go

Note: Discuss other treasures and other dragons in your life and create some new verses of your own.

Relaxation Breathing

Purpose: calm your body and mind

Sit comfortably and close your eyes.

Become aware of your breath.

Focus your attention on your belly as you breathe in and out.

Place one hand on your belly and notice how it rises and falls.

Focus your attention on your chest as you breathe in and out.

Place the other hand on your chest and notice how it rises and falls.

Now let your hands come to rest in your lap.

As you breathe into your belly, count 1 - 2 - 3 - 4.

As you breathe into your chest, count 5 - 6 - 7 - 8.

As you let all the air out, count 8 - 7 - 6 - 5 - 4 - 3 - 2 - 1.

Practice this relaxation breathing a few more times by yourself.

Now breathe in and out in time with this verse:

> I fill my belly, then my chest
> (on the inhaling breath to a count of 8 syllables)

> I now release, relax, and rest
> (on the exhaling breath to a count of 8 syllables)

You may want to hold your breath as you pause slightly between each line.

Practice this relaxation breathing a few minutes every day.

Use it especially when you are tense or excited.

At nighttime, exhale very, very slowly to help you fall asleep easily.

Be Still, Be Still

Purpose: feel centered and quiet inside

Sit comfortably and close your eyes.

Be aware of your breathing.

Notice the muscles of your face.

Let go of any tightness around your eyes and cheeks and jaw.

Notice the muscles of your neck and shoulders.

Let go of your shoulders as you breathe out.

Feel relaxation flowing in and out, gently and easily.

Continue to breathe quietly.

As you listen to this poem, breathe in on one line, breathe out on the next:

> Be still, be still (inhale)
> And let your breath be slow (exhale)
> Be still, be still
> Let all your worries go.

Be still, be still
Let tension disappear
Be still, be still
Releasing all your fear.

Be still, be still
Let go of daily care
Be still, be still
And simply be aware.

Be still, be still
Let all your hurry cease
Be still, be still
And rest awhile in peace.

(to be used at rest time and bedtime)

Be still, be still
And let your breath be deep
Be still, be still
And gently fall asleep.

I Am Still

Purpose: relax with quiet breathing and images of nature

Sit comfortably and close your eyes.

Listen to your quiet breathing.

Imagine sitting on a beautiful beach on a warm summer day.

Feel the sun shining down on your body.

Notice the blueness of the sky overhead.

Watch a palm tree swaying gracefully in the tropical breeze.

Listen to the sound of the ocean waves rolling onto the sand.

Let your breath move to each line of the following
poem:

> I am still, I breathe in 1 (inhale)
> I'm warm and glowing like the sun (exhale)
>
> I am still, I breathe in 2
> I'm open like the sky of blue
>
> I am still, I breathe in 3
> I'm strong and grounded like a tree
>
> I am still, I breathe in 4
> I flow like waves upon the shore
>
> I am still, I breathe in 5
> My total being is alive!
>
> As I'm breathing 6 and 7
> I feel peace from earth and heaven.

Moving

Milkshake

Purpose: relax your whole body

Stand with your feet comfortably apart.

Think about your favorite milkshake.

Imagine that you are a kitchen blender.

Pretend you have a cup of milk in one hand.

Pour it into the opening at the top of your head.

Now with the other hand add a little vanilla.

Put in some slices of your favorite fruit.

Add a scoop of cold ice cream.

What else would you like to add to your milkshake?

Now take two fingers of one hand and plug the electric cord into the wall.

Take the thumb of your other hand and press your belly button on.

Now SHAKE! Feel all the ingredients blending together.

Shake yourself very well until everything is smooth and creamy.

Make the sound of a whirling blender.

When the milkshake is ready, turn the motor off.

Imagine taking a long cool drink of your special treat.

Offer to share some with a friend.

Body Bopper Machine

Purpose: energize and relax your whole body.

Stand comfortably with your legs and arms relaxed.

Imagine that you are going to visit your favorite health club.

As you walk in the door you notice some new exercise machines.

They are designed to energize and relax your whole body.

You decide to try out each one:

HEAD TAPPER — bounce your fingers lightly on your head and neck

SCALP SCRATCHER — give yourself a shampoo with your fingers

CHEEK SLAPPER — slap the tips of your fingers against your cheeks

EAR TUGGER — pull gently on the tops of your ears as though you were raising your antennae

SHOULDER SQUEEZER — lace your fingers behind your head and press your elbows back

WING FLAPPER — place your hands on your shoulders and flap your elbows up and down and around in circles

CHEST STRETCHER — clasp your hands together behind your seat and bend forward as you lift up your arms

RIB POUNDER — pound your elbows against the sides of your waist as you shift your weight from one foot to the other

FINGER FLICKER — open and close your fists as fast as you can

ARM FLINGER — fling one arm at a time around in a big circle

BELLY THUMPER — thump your belly with the palms of your hands

SEAT SPANKER — give yourself some taps on the seat with both hands

BACK BUMPER — use your fists to pound up and down along the sides of your spine

TAIL WAGGER — wiggle your tail like a puppy coming out of the ocean

KNEE KNOCKER — lift one knee at a time to meet the opposite fist

FOOT STOMPER — kick one foot up at a time to the outside and touch the palms of your hands

BODY BOPPER MACHINE — turn on lots of machines at the same time and let everything happen at once!

Spaghetti Dance

Purpose: shake your whole body

Stand with your feet comfortably apart.

Imagine spaghetti before it has been cooked.

Let your body become stiff and straight like raw, hard spaghetti.

In front of you is a large cooking pot of bubbling water.

Let the spaghetti JUMP into the pot.

Feel the heat of the water.

Begin to feel yourself becoming softer and softer.

Feel the water bubbling all around you.

Dance around inside the pot.

Feel all the spaghetti becoming limp.

All the stiffness is boiling away.

When dinner is ready, imagine being served onto a warm plate.

Let the spaghetti fall down into a pile.

Feel yourself letting go completely.

Puppy Dog Wiggle

Purpose: let go of tightness

Stand with your feet comfortably apart.

Imagine a puppy dog swimming in a lake.

Watch him come toward shore and jump onto the land.

Pretend you are that puppy wanting to get dry.

Shake your head dry.

Shake all the water off your body.

Shake your front legs.

Shake your tail.

Now shake your whole body.

You are still not quite dry yet.

Wiggle your tail again.

Feel the water spraying all around you

Now change yourself into a surfer.

Grab your towel and dry off your shoulders.

Dry off your hips.

Shake your feet dry.

Now lie down on the soft sand and relax in the warm sunshine.

Roller Coaster

Purpose: balance and coordination

Sit on the carpet with the bottoms of your feet together.

Be sure there is plenty of room around you.

Hold on to both feet with both hands.

Rock from side to side.

Let each knee touch the floor.

Push yourself onto one knee and then over onto your shoulder and across your upper back.

Continue to swing around in a full circle several times.

Press your elbows against your legs if you need a push.

Return to a sitting position.

Now roll around in the opposite direction.

Be sure to swing sideways onto your knee and shoulder so you can make a complete circle.

Imagine a roller coaster going up and down, round and around.

When you are able to roll easily, sit back to back with a partner or in a group of four.

Decide on a starting signal and roll around in the same direction.

Look over your shoulder and watch each other for timing.

Be sure to laugh at yourselves!

Hello Body

Purpose: wake yourself up

Stand with your feet comfortably apart.

Shake one hand and say, "Hello hand." Now say "Hello" to the other hand.

Shake one foot and say, "Hello foot."

Say "Hello" to the other foot.

Shake and say "Hello" to your hips.

Continue to shake and say:

> "Hello seat."
>
> "Hello belly."
>
> "Hello knees."
>
> "Hello elbows."
>
> "Hello shoulders."

Wiggle your nose and say "Hello" to it.

Flap your ears with your fingers and say "Hello."

Say "Hello" to any part of your body you want to shake.

Everyone say "Hello" out loud at the same time.

Now say "Hello" to your whole body at once.

Are you feeling wide awake?

Now say "Hello" to a friend nearby.

Go, Drakely, Go!

Purpose: release energy while having fun in a group

Stand in groups of three to five or in a large circle with one person behind the other like a train.

Place your hands on the waist of the person in front of you and sing to the tune of "Dry Bones."

Drakely the Dragon has eight legs
> (Kick right leg to the side four times.)

Drakely the Dragon has eight legs
> (Kick left leg to the side four times.)

Drakely the Dragon has eight legs
> (Jump forward twice and backwards twice.)

Go, Drakely, go!
> (Wave both hands in the air while the person at the head of the line runs around to the end.)

Place your hands on the waist of the person in front of you and continue with the next verse.

Drakely the Dragon has seven legs etc.

On each verse continue decreasing the number from eight to one.

On the last verse wiggle your hips from side to side in time with the music while singing:

Drakely the Dragon has no legs

Drakely the Dragon has no legs

Drakely the Dragon has no legs

Drakely is a snake!
> (Wave both hands in the air and rotate your body.)

Imagining and Creating

At Dawn

Purpose: calming the mind

Lie down in a comfortable position and close your eyes.

Imagine yourself at the edge of a quiet mountain lake.

It is very early in the morning.

All is silent, all is still.

The surface of the water is like a shining mirror.

Your mind is like that lake, completely quiet, completely calm.

As the first rays of sunlight appear, the world is beginning to wake up.

Listen to the call of a mourning dove in the distance.

Feel a gentle breeze dancing across your face.

Notice a leaf blowing onto the surface of the water.

Tiny ripples are beginning to circle out in all directions.

The ripples on the lake are like the thoughts floating through your mind.

Notice them... and let them go.

(long pause)

Now bring your attention back to the quiet lake.
All is silent, all is still.
The lake is completely clear.
And your mind is in a quiet state of peace.
Listen to a soft voice within in you saying...

> I calm my mind and let it be
> Filled with strength and clarity.

At Midday

Purpose: calming the body

Imagine yourself at the edge of a quiet mountain lake.

It is midday.

The sun is high in the sky.

The surface of the water is stirred by gentle breezes.

The sun is shining down upon your face and neck.

It is warming your shoulders.

Feel a wave of sunshine flowing down through your arms from your shoulders... to your elbows...

to your wrists... to your palms...

and out through the tips of your fingers.

Feel the warmth flowing down from your neck...

to your chest... around your lungs...

and into your heart.

With each breath, let the sunshine melt into your whole body.

(long pause)

Now bring your attention back to the quiet lake.

All is silent, all is still.

The sun is warm and relaxing.

And your body is in a quiet state of peace.

Listen to a soft voice within you saying...

> I rest my body, let it be
> Filled with healing energy

At Twilight

Purpose: calming the heart

Imagine yourself at the edge of a quiet mountain lake.

It is early evening.

The sun is disappearing behind the pink and purple clouds.

All is silent, all is still.

The surface of the water reflects the colors of the sunset.

gold... orange... turquoise... violet.

As you breathe, imagine that the air around you is becoming one of those colors.

Inhale that color into your lungs.

Let it flow into your heart.

Let it fill you with radiance and beauty.

Breathe away your sadness and loneliness.

Let the colors of the sunset glow inside of you.
Let them fill you with love and joy.
With each breath, let go a little more.
(long pause)
Now bring your attention back to the quiet lake.
All is silent, all is still.
The colors of the sky are glowing.
And your heart is in a quiet state of peace.
Listen to a soft voice within you saying...

> I still my heart and let it be
> Filled with love and harmony.

At Midnight

Purpose: calming the spirit

Imagine yourself at the edge of a quiet mountain lake.

It is midnight, and the air is cool.

The dark sky is sprinkled with millions of stars.

The moon is playing hide-and-seek with the clouds.

All is silent, all is still.

The surface of the water reflects the sparkling jewels of heaven.

As you look out into the open expanse above you, your thoughts soar into the distance...

beyond the clouds... beyond the atmosphere...

beyond the moon... and the planets...

and the solar system.

You feel expanded... lifted up...

transported beyond time... and space.

You are sailing as far as your imagination can carry you.

You are connected with the whole universe.
(long pause)
Now bring your attention back to the quiet lake.
All is silent, all is still.
The sky above goes on forever... and forever.
And your spirit is in a quiet state of peace.
Listen to a soft voice within you saying...

> I free my spirit, let it be
> Filled with deep serenity.

If You Were a Dragon

Purpose: stimulate creative imagination

Note: This activity is especially fun to do using dragon puppets. Simple ones can be made from paper bags or children's socks.

Below are some questions to ask the dragons:

If you were an adventurous dragon, where would you like to go?

If you were a playful dragon, in what ways would you like to have fun?

If you were a hungry dragon, what would you like to eat? (Encourage unusual responses such as bumblebee ice cream, daffodil soup, spaghetti and mudballs, petunia pizza, etc.)

If you were a peace loving dragon, what would you suggest to the leaders of the world'

If you were a magic dragon, how would you use your power to help other people?

If you were an invisible dragon, what would you do to be kind to others in secret?

If you were a pet dragon, to whom would you like to belong?

If you were a busy dragon, what would you do to relax at the end of the day?

If you were a healthy dragon, how would you take good care of yourself?

If you were a creative dragon, what would you invent that would be helpful to the world?

If you were a wealthy dragon, what worthwhile project would you support?

If you were a very smart dragon, what world problem would you help to solve?

If you were a funny dragon, what would you do to make people laugh?

If you were a very wise dragon, what would you teach to the children of the world?

Your Own Special Dragon

Purpose: enhance creativity and self expression

Note: Make a collection of "beautiful junk" including pipe cleaners, paper clips, rubber bands, Styrofoam, aluminum foil, bottle caps, tongue depressors, corks, toothpicks, toilet paper tubes, buttons, string, etc. Have available scissors, tape, glue, and a stapler.

Imagine that you are exploring an enchanted forest.

Or perhaps you have just landed on another planet.

A very unusual creature appears before your eyes.

You blink your eyes and look again.

You see a dragon with some very strange features.

This dragon looks different from any other dragon in the world.

This dragon tells you about a difficult problem or fear.

This dragon tells you about some special magical powers.

This dragon whispers a secret in your ear.

You invite the dragon to come home with you for a visit.

Use the "beautiful junk" to create your own special dragon.

Take as much time as you need.

After the dragons have been created, introduce them to everyone in the group.

Ask the dragons some of the following questions:

> What is your name?
>
> What unusual food do you like to eat?
>
> What magical power do you have?
>
> What is your most difficult problem right now?
>
> Is there anything that you are afraid of?

Ask the creator of each dragon some of the following questions:

> Is your dragon willing to tell us a secret?
>
> How will your dragon be helpful to you at home?
>
> Where is your dragon going to sleep at your house?
>
> How long do you think your dragon will live with you?

Somewhere Over the Rainbow

Purpose: feel energized and relaxed

Sit comfortably with your hands resting on your knees.

Turn your palms upward and close your eyes.

Imagine a rainbow in the sky above you.

Notice how clear and bright the colors are.

Now imagine creating your own rainbow to hold in your hands.

Pretend you have a magic paintbrush.

Beginning with the color red, paint the first stripe of your rainbow.
Let it curve up from one hand and down into the other.
Notice how this red stripe is glowing with energy.
It helps you feel very alive and awake.

(long pause)

Now paint a stripe of orange underneath the red.
Let it move from one hand to the other.
The orange stripe is warm and glowing.
You feel comfortable and relaxed.

(long pause)

With your magic brush, paint a stripe of yellow.
Let it glow like the sunshine.
It is bright and clear like daffodils.
You feel strong and confident.

(long pause)

As you paint your stripe of green, picture a grassy meadow.

Imagine being surrounded by green energy in the springtime.
Green is a healthy color.
You feel happy and balanced.

(long pause)

Imagine looking up at the sky and finding a clear shade of blue.
Now paint a band of blue in your rainbow.
Let it stretch from one hand to the other.
Feel the openness and peace of the blue sky.

(long pause)

Now picture the color indigo - a dark bluish purple.
Paint a band of indigo underneath the blue.
Let your attention be directed inside.
Notice how deeply quiet you feel.

(long pause)

Take your brush again and paint a stripe of violet.
Put violet along the bottom of your rainbow.
Notice how pure and gentle this color is.
Feel how perfectly still you are inside.

(long pause)

Now begin to play with your rainbow.
Move one hand up and the other hand down.
Feel its energy flowing from one hand into the other.
Open your eyes and wrap your rainbow around your neck.

Roll some of it into a ball and toss it to a friend.

Wrap some more of your rainbow around the neck of someone nearby.

Sack of Sand

Purpose: let go of tightness

Lie down comfortably and close your eyes.

Imagine that you are lying in your backyard on a warm summer afternoon.

Feel the weight of your body sinking into the earth.

Feel yourself getting heavier and heavier like a sack of sand.

Feel the weight of the sand upon the ground.

Imagine that there is a small hole in the bottom of the sack.

Let the sand trickle out through

your big toes.

Feel your feet becoming loose and limp.

Let the sand trickle away from your ankles.

Let the sand disappear from your lower legs and knees.

Let it move away from your upper legs and seat.

Feel the sack of sand becoming empty.

Let more sand trickle out with each outgoing breath.

Let the sand move away from your belly and hips.

The bottom half of the sack is completely empty now.

Feel how loose and limp you are.

Now let the sand trickle out through the ends of your fingers.

Feel it move away from your arms and shoulders.

Feel it disappear from your chest.

The sack of sand is almost empty now.

Feel how loose you are as you lie limply on the ground.

Enjoy that feeling of emptiness and relaxation.

Melting Candle

Purpose: relax your whole body

Lie down comfortably and close your eyes.

Imagine that you are stretched out in the sun on a warm day.

Your body is made of wax.

You are like a huge candle.

As the sun shines, your toes begin to melt.

Then your feet and ankles begin to melt.

Feel the warm sun on your legs.

Your knees are melting ...

and then your thighs.

Your seat and hips begin to melt.

Your lower body is soft and warm.

Feel your fingers melting into the grass.

Then your hands and wrists melt away.

Your elbows begin to melt...

and then your shoulders.

Feel the warm sun on your chest and neck.

Let your whole body melt into the earth.

You are completely relaxed and comfortable.

You are completely at peace.

Special Delivery

Purpose: imagine something very pleasant

Sit comfortably and close your eyes.

Pretend that you are alone in your own living room.

The mailman is on his way to your house.

Listen to his footsteps on the front walk.

Hear him put some letters in your mailbox.

Watch him walk away from your house.

Go get the mail.

There is a special delivery letter addressed to you.

Sit down and open it.

Notice how you are feeling right now.

Inside the letter is some very good news for you.

There is a wonderful surprise.

Something special is going to happen soon.

Find out what it is.

Now how are you feeling?

Breathe in deeply and open your eyes very slowly.

Tell someone about your good news.

Warm Waterfall

Purpose: feel warm all over

Note: You may want to do this
stretch as you listen to quiet music.

Stand with your feet comfortably apart.

Imagine a warm spring of water rising up from the
earth.

Breathe in and slowly lift your arms up in front of you.

Stretch your arms overhead.

Imagine a warm waterfall of energy coming down from
above.

Breathe out and lower your arms to your sides.

Relax and rest.

Continue to stretch your arms up as you breathe in ...

and down as you breathe out.

Feel the energy of the spring rising up through your
body and out the top of your head.

Feel the energy of the waterfall floating down over your
body and into your feet.

Close your eyes and imagine the water flowing inside
of you... and outside of you.

Butterfly Wings

Purpose: feel still inside

Lie down comfortably and close your eyes.

Imagine that you are relaxing in a meadow on a warm day.

Notice the color of the summer sky overhead.

Feel the soft grass under your body.

Watch the fluffy clouds floating by.

Breathe in and smell the pine trees in the air.

Feel a cool summer breeze on your face.

Listen to the insects in the grass.

Smell the wild flowers and the clover.

Feel the warm sunshine all over your body.

Listen to the chirping of the birds in the trees.

Watch a giant butterfly nearby.

Notice the colors of its wings in the sunlight.

See how gently it moves.

It is about to land on your knee.

Lie very still.

It will stay right there if you're quiet.

Now the butterfly wants to rest on your shoulder.

Be very still.

Breathe very gently.

Enjoy being peaceful together.

Shhh...let the butterfly go to sleep.

Dragon Treasure Chest

Purpose: enhance self-esteem

Note: Make a dragon treasure chest by placing a mirror inside of a box. A shoe box works well or a box with a hinged lid. You may want to decorate the outside with pictures of dragons.

Dragons are sometimes in charge of protecting precious treasures.

Dragons guard the entrances to temples and caves.

They make sure that the valuable treasures are safe.

Inside each of us are some other kinds of treasures.

One of our most important treasures is our health.

We need to protect our health to keep it strong.

Some other precious treasures are intelligence, creativity, and humor.

What are some of the precious treasures inside of you? What are the special treasures in your heart?

Have you thought about music? laughter? peace? joy?

What do you think is the most important treasure of all?

When you look inside the Dragon Treasure Chest, you will see something very precious and important.

You will see a special treasure.

When you know what it is, don't tell anyone.

Keep it a surprise for the next person to see.

Now come and look inside the Dragon Treasure Chest.

Do you agree that this is one of the greatest treasures in the world?

Rainbow Breathing

Purpose: feel balanced and relaxed

Sit comfortably and close your eyes.
Let your hands rest easily on your lap.
Let your breath flow gently in and out.

Put your attention into your seat.
Imagine that you are sitting on a red velvet cushion.
As you breathe in, let red energy flow into the base of
    your spine.
Feel red energy and health flowing inside of you.

Put your attention into your belly.
Imagine that you are wearing some orange shorts.
As you breathe in, let orange energy flow into your belly.
Feel energy and warmth flowing inside of you.

Put your attention just above your belly button.
Imagine tying a yellow silk scarf around your waist.
As you breathe in, let yellow energy flow into your
    middle.
Feel yellow energy and strength flowing inside of you.

Put your attention into your chest.
Imagine that you are wearing a green shirt.
Breathe in, let green energy flow into your heart.
Feel green energy and love glowing inside of you.

Put your attention into the base of your throat.
Imagine wearing a light blue scarf around your neck.
Breathe in, let blue energy flow into your throat.
Feel blue energy and peace flowing inside of you.

Put your attention into the middle of your forehead.
Imagine you are wearing an indigo (dark blue)
    headband.
As you breathe in, let indigo energy flow into your
    thoughts.
Feel indigo energy and wisdom flowing inside of you.

Put your attention into the top of your head.
Imagine you are wearing a crown of violet jewels.
As you breathe in, let violet energy flow into your
    head.
Feel violet energy and trust flowing inside your whole
    being.

Now imagine that you can breathe from the base of
    your spine to the top of your head.
Feel all the colors of the rainbow inside you.
Imagine yourself being wrapped in light and peace.

Let's Pretend

Purpose: develop imagination

Pretend you are a blossom
Glistening with dew
Paint your petals lavender,
Violet and blue.

Now become a baby deer
Learning how to run
Change into a unicorn
Leaping in the sun.

Pretend you are a bunny
Wriggling your nose
Turn into a butterfly
Resting on a rose.

Pretend you are a seashell
Tossed upon the sand
Listen to the ocean breeze
Drifting toward the land.

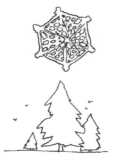

Now become a gentle wave
Splashing on the shore
Turn into a graceful gull
Learning how to soar.

You can be a golden fish
Swimming in a dream
Glide beneath the waterfalls
Of a mountain stream.

Now become a fluffy cloud
Floating in the sky
Change into a snowflake
Gently dancing by.

Be a ray of sunshine
Full of warmth and light
Be a silver moonbeam
Glowing in the night.

You can be a rainbow
Magical to see
Close your eyes and you'll become
What you want to be.

Listening

You Are the Ocean

Purpose: listen to your breathing

Sit comfortably and close your eyes.

Let go of your cheeks and jaw.

Let go of your shoulders and elbows.

Imagine that you are at the beach in the summertime.

(long pause)

Feel the warm sunshine on your face.

Smell the salt air.

Taste the salt on your lips.

Feel the cool ocean breeze on your skin.

Listen to the sound of your breathing.

(long pause)

As you breathe in, see the waves roll in.

As you breathe out, hear the waves roll out.

Feel your breath flowing with the ocean.

Feel the rhythm of the waves.

Let the sunshine soak into your body.

Be at peace with the waves.

Be at peace with your breathing.

Become one with the ocean.

Magic Messages

Purpose: feel good about yourself

Relax in whatever way you are most comfortable.

Close your eyes and let go of your cheeks and jaw.

Let go of your chin and tongue.

Let your eyes roll up toward the top
of your head, like marbles.

Listen to your breathing.

(long pause)

Repeat these messages quietly to yourself...

    My legs are heavy and warm.

    My arms are quiet and still.

    My heartbeat is steady and even.

    My breathing is slow and deep.

    My forehead is cool.

    My whole body is comfortable.

    I am calm and relaxed.

    I am peaceful inside.

    I feel healthy and strong.

    I can remember what I learn.

    I can take good care of myself.

    I can make friends easily.

    I am a very special person in my family.

Think of other messages which are important to you.

Repeat them quietly to yourself.

Know that these messages are true.

Animal Guide

Purpose: self awareness

Sit comfortably and close your eyes.

Pretend that you are at the edge of a meadow.

Notice what is growing there... notice what is moving.

You see a baby animal coming out of the bushes.

He begins walking in your direction.

He looks very tame and friendly.

Notice what color he is... notice what size he is.

Watch him move very slowly toward you.

Put your hand out to welcome him.

Feel his soft nose against your fingers.

Find something in your pocket for him to eat.

Touch him... pet him... feel his soft warm body.

How does it feel to have a new friend?

(long pause)

This animal is very wise.

He knows a lot about the forest ...

He knows a lot about life.

He wants to tell you a secret about you.

He wants to whisper it in your ear.

He wants to tell you something special about yourself.

Listen to what he is saying.

(long pause)

Ask him a question about yourself.

(long pause)

Now listen to his answer.

Remember... this animal is very wise.

Who do you think this animal really is?

Music in the Trees

Purpose: develop sense of hearing

Relax in whatever way you are the most comfortable.

Close your eyes and pretend that you are camping in the forest.

The sun is just beginning to come up.

The air is getting warmer.

Listen to the sounds around you.

(long pause)

A bee is buzzing in the dandelions.

A cricket is chirping in the grass.

A chipmunk is scurrying across a log.

A squirrel is chewing on an acorn.

Some blue jays are chattering in the bushes.

What other sounds can you hear?

(long pause)

Some fairies are hiding under the mushrooms.

They are playing their violins.

Some elves are sitting on top of the buttercups.

They are playing their magical harps.

Some leprechauns are perched on a tree stump.

They all have tiny flutes.

A goblin is tapping on a tree stump.

Listen to the orchestra!

What other instruments can you hear?

Pretend that you are the conductor of this woodland symphony.

Listen to the music in the trees!

What Can You Hear?

Purpose: self awareness

Lie down comfortably and close your eyes.

Say your own name quietly to yourself.

Hear your name echo softly inside your head.

Pretend that you can hear your hair growing.

Listen to your breathing.

(long pause)

Hear the breath at the back of your throat.

Listen to your heartbeat.

(long pause)

Hear the blood flowing like a tiny stream.

Feel your chest moving as you breathe.

(long pause)

Hear the air as it leaves your lungs.

Imagine that you can listen inside from the back of your belly button.

What sounds can you hear?

(long pause)

Imagine that you can listen outside with the tips of your fingers.

What sounds can you bring back into your hands?

(long pause)

Imagine that you can pick up sounds with the bottom of your toes.

How do your feet feel?

(long pause)

Pretend that you can hear your toenails growing.

Pretend that you can listen to the world around you through the holes of your skin.

What can you hear now?

Touching

Human Drum

Purpose: feel good all over

Stand with your feet comfortably apart.

Pretend that your body is a drum and you can play it with your hands.

Tap your fingertips on the top of your head.

Tap your fingertips on your cheeks.

Slap your palms up and down your arms.

Pound your fists on your chest and make some drumming sounds.

Hit your elbows against your ribs.

Slap your hands against your belly.

Pound your fists on your hips.

Decide how hard you want to play your drum.

What feels good to you?

Spank yourself gently on your seat.

Pound your fists up and down your lower back.

Pound your fists on your opposite knees.

What other part of your drum would you like to play?

Ask some friends if they would like you to play on their drums.

Ask them to play on yours.

Raindrops

Purpose: help another person feel good

Stand next to a partner.

As your partner bends forward from the waist, rest your hands gently on the back.

Pretend that your fingertips are like raindrops.

Tap lightly up and down the back between the neck and the seat.

Tap across the top of the shoulders.

Now let your raindrops fall gently on the head.

Ask your partner how that feels.

If your partner would like more pressure, let your raindrops become hailstones.

Again ask your partner how that feels.

Only do what feels comfortable.

Now change places with your partner.

When you are done, thank each other for the wonderful presents you have just received.

Let's Go for a Walk

Purpose: help another person relax (especially at bedtime)

Ask your partner to lie face down on the floor or bed.

Kneel or sit beside your partner and place your hands on the back.

As you tell the following story, illustrate it with your hands.

One day I was walking near the edge of a beautiful green meadow.

(Make large circles on the back with both hands.)

At the edge of the meadow a mountain stream trickled.

(Run the side of your hand down the back in a wavy line.)

Some rabbits were jumping about in the grass.

(Tap your fingers lightly all over the back.)

A snake slithered across the meadow toward the bushes.

(Draw a wavy line with your fingertips.)

The warm sunshine shone brightly on everything in the forest.

(Slide your palms around the upper back and shoulders.)

Continue the story with your own images and hand movements.

What other kinds of stories can you make up and illustrate? How about an underwater adventure or a trip into outer space?

Fabulous Feet

Purpose: help another person's feet feel good

Both you and your partner remove shoes.

Ask your partner to lie face down on the floor with legs out straight.

Stand at the end of the feet and place your toes on top of your partner's toes.

Gently begin walking your feet up the bottom of your partner's feet.

Press down on the inside and the outside of the arches.

Ask how that feels.

If your partner would like more pressure, step a little harder.

Only do what feels comfortable.

Now turn around and place your heels on top of your partner's toes.

Gently begin walking backwards up the bottom of the feet.

Again ask your partner how that feels.

Now change places and enjoy having your partner walk gently on your feet.

Let your partner know how that feels to you.

You now have a very special gift to share with a friend!

Energy Elbows

Purpose: help another person's back feel good

Note: This activity is especially good to share with parents and children together at home.

Form a group of three people and number off.

#1: kneel down, rest your hips on your ankles, and place your head on the floor.

#2: kneel down and face the seat of #1.

#3: kneel down and face the head of #1.

#2 and #3: clasp your own hands together and place your elbows in the center of the back of #1.

#2 and #3: gently pull your arms back toward your bodies as you press your elbows into your partner's back.

Imagine sending energy all along the spine from the shoulders to the tailbone.

Ask #1 how that feels.

Continue to work together for a few minutes, so #1 receives comfortable pressure wherever it is wanted.

When you are done, rotate positions so that all three partners have a turn.

Rhymes and Rhythms

Talk Your Walk

Purpose: use positive affirmations in time with your footsteps and your breath

Note: This activity is good to do when you are on a walk by yourself.

As you walk along at a comfortable pace, be aware of your breathing.

Also be aware of your footsteps.

Gradually let your footsteps and your breath come together.

Breathe in to a count of 8 steps.

Breathe out to a count of 8 steps.

When you are comfortable with this rhythm, begin to say these verses to yourself (silently or out loud) as you walk and breathe:

With every step more strength I gain
      (inhale for 8 steps)

As I let go of all my pain
      (exhale for 8 steps)

With every step more strength I feel
As I allow myself to heal

I breathe the air, I feel the sun
I'm ready for a day of fun!

For special needs, substitute other words such as:

With every step more strength I gain
As I release my headache pain

With every step more strength I feel
As I allow my arm to heal

I flow with health, I breathe with ease
As I release my allergies

Balance is my daily goal
In mind and body, heart and soul

With every step more strength I find
Within my body/spirit/mind

Dragons, Dragons, in the Sky

Purpose: coordinate auditory visual and kinesthetic learning, sung to the tune of "Twinkle Twinkle Little Star"

> Dragons, dragons in the sky
> Why don't I have wings to fly?
> Up into the sky so blue
> All around the world with you
> Dragons, dragons in the sky
> Why don't I have wings to fly?

Words	Motions
Dragons, dragons	Open and close fingers against thumb two times (like a dragon's mouth)
in the sky	Point index fingers up at the sky two times
Why don't I	Point to yourself two times
have wings to fly?	Flap elbows up and down two times (like wings)
Up into the sky so blue	Raise arms overhead and open in a wide circle
All around the world	Rotate one hand around the other in front of body
with you	Point one index finger toward another person
Dragons, dragons	Open and close fingers against thumb two times
in the sky	Point index fingers up at the sky two times
Why don't I	Point to yourself two times
have wings to fly?	Flap elbows up and down two times

Each time you sing the song, leave out one line of words but continue to do the hand motions.

Keep the same rhythm going so that at the end everyone is doing the hand motions in unison without any words.

Way Down Yonder

Purpose: release excessive energy and establish a quiet mood

Sit so your palms can rest comfortably on your knees. Establish a four-beat rhythm with your hands:

1. slap your hands on your knees
2. clap your hands together in front of you
3. snap the fingers of your left hand
4. snap the fingers of your right hand

For very young children you may simplify the pattern:

1. slap your hands on your knees
2. slap your hands on your knees
3. clap your hands together in front of you
4. clap your hands together in front of you

Chant the following verse, continuing the rhythm with your hands on the first three lines. On the fourth line, maintain the rhythm but change the gestures:

On the word "head," put both thumbs up in the air

On the word "tail," point both thumbs down

On the word "off," move both hands palms down in a straight line in front of you.

> Way down yonder not so very far off
>
> My dragon caught the whooping cough
>
> He whooped so hard with the whooping cough
>
> That he whooped his head and his tail right off

Chant the verse with the gestures six times, each time changing the volume of the chant and the energy of the gestures:

1. a little louder with energetic gestures
2. even louder with more energetic gestures
3. very loud with extremely vigorous gestures
4. softer with less vigorous gestures
5. very soft with small gestures
6. in a whisper with tiny gestures

Nine Little Dragons

Purpose: a good activity to use before rest time or bedtime or to bring the energy level of a group way down and into a quiet space

Note: Use dragon puppets if they are available or use your hands to imitate the dragons. As you sing, use appropriate hand motions to go with the words.

Tune: "Ten Little Indians" (very lively)

One little, two little, three little dragons.
Four little, five little, six little dragons
Seven little, eight little, nine little dragons
All came out to play.

They jumped on my knee, they flew through the air
They started dancing in my hair
And now they're running everywhere
'Cause dragons love to play.

(very slowly and softly)

Nine little, eight little, seven little dragons
Six little, five little, four little dragons
Three little, two little, one little dragon
They don't want to play.

They've been having so much fun
Now they're sleeping in the sun
They're so tired, every one
Sh... Sh... Sh...

The Dragon Thermometer

Dragon Thermometer

___

5. OUT OF CONTROL

4. BUSY

3. CENTERED

2. PEACEFUL

1. WORN OUT

___

Using the Dragon Thermometer

Note: Photocopy the Dragon Thermometer, enlarging it as much as possible. Glue it to tag board. Cut slits at the horizontal lines, making them wide enough for the yarn "mercury" to easily slide through them. Tie two lengths of yarn together: one red, one white. Slide the ends of the yarn through the slits and tie them together on the back of the thermometer forming a continuous loop. Be sure the knots are strong so they won't separate when the yarn is repeatedly slid up and down.

Several years ago, I was directing a relaxation program called The Hang Loose Club for 22 children and 8 adults at an elementary school in Denver

I had just started using my Dragon Thermometer as a tool for helping children take more responsibility for their own behavior.

Along with the thermometer, each child had a chart on which to keep a weekly record of their energy at four different times during the day: morning, noon, afternoon, and evening. Later we discussed what they had observed about themselves, including the time of the day when their energies were the highest and lowest.

One 4th grade boy was especially interested in this project. His mother told me one day that her son was carrying his chart around in his jeans pocket. She overhead him saying, "Let's see now, I'm heading toward 5 and I'd rather be a 3. What can I do to relax myself?"

A first grade teacher told me that after using the Dragon Thermometer in her classroom for a while, she heard one child say to another, "Sally, you seem like a 1 today. I like to play with you much more when you are a 3."

I have found the Dragon Thermometer to be a useful way of identifying children's behavior without labeling the child. It helps children learn that they can be more in charge of their feelings and their actions.

Parents have reported to me that they have Dragon Thermometers of their own, which they put on the refrigerator to let the rest of the family know how they are feeling. Some children I know hang their thermometers on their bedroom doors.

While teaching in a language arts program for gifted preschool children at the University for Youth in Denver, I had been using the Dragon Thermometer for several days but was not sure if the concept had really sunk in yet.

One day the children were going to appear on a radio program. By the time they arrived at the radio station, they were acting like "dreadful dragons." One of the teachers simply reached up in the air as if to grab onto a string at the top of the thermometer and said, "Okay, dragons, let's get centered." At that point, the children reached up for their own imaginary strings and pulled them down to center while making an oo-oo sound, sliding down from a high to a moderate pitch.

Within moments the class was settled down and ready to be interviewed.

How simple!

Dragon Thermometer Songs

Purpose: reinforce the message of the Dragon Thermometer

Note: Photocopy the Dragon Thermometer, enlarging it as much as possible, and post it for all to see.

Tune: All the Little Ducklings

> I'm a dreadful dragon
> Noisy as can be
> > When I shout
> > I need TIME OUT
> So I can get control of me
>
> I'm a droopy dragon
> Tired as can be
> > I know it's best
> > For me to rest
> So I can have more energy
>
> I'm a centered dragon
> Happy as can be
> > Relaxed is how
> > I'm feeling now
> Come on along and play with me!

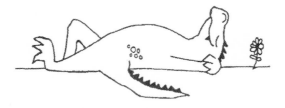

Tune: Ten Little Indians

Once I met a dreadful dragon
Always noisy, always braggin'
I'm not like that dreadful dragon
No, that's not like me

Once I met a droopy dragon (very slowly)
Always tired, always laggin'
I'm not like that droopy dragon
No, that's not like me.

I'm a calm and centered dragon
Happy when my tail is waggin'
I can be that centered dragon
Yes, that's just like me!

Sharing Touch

Weather Report

Purpose: release tension in the upper back and shoulders

Ask a partner to sit cross-legged on the floor.

Kneel down and place your hands comfortably on your partner's shoulders from behind.

Begin tapping your fingers lightly along the top of the shoulders.

Extend these gently falling snowflakes up the back of the neck to the top of the head.

Change the snowflakes into raindrops tapping a little harder on the head, neck and shoulders.

Let the raindrops become hailstones, flicking your wrists as you let your fingertips bounce a little harder.

Ask your partner if that feels okay.

Now create some thunder. Cup your hands and clap them across the shoulders and down along the top of the arms.

Next comes the lightning. Use the sides of your hands with a chopping motion against the shoulders and upper back.

Use your thumbs like the eye of a tornado. Press into the muscles with small deep circles. Find out where your partner would like the tornado to land.

Now for the meteor shower. Make fists and move up

and down the back along either side of the spinal column.

Prepare for the earthquake. Hold onto your partner's upper arms and gently shake the whole upper body.

Get ready for the tidal wave Place your palms on the upper back and move them vigorously from the shoulders down to the waist. Imagine waves sloshing all up and down the coast.

Now the storm is over.

Feel the calm as you place your hands gently on your partner's shoulders and rest.

Send warmth into the muscles as you imagine soothing energy flowing out of your hands into the body.

Very gradually lift your hands several inches above your partner's shoulders.

Hold them there for a few seconds.

Then lower your hands to your sides and shake them gently.

All during the Weather Report, check to be sure that your partner is comfortable and enjoying the activity.

Adjust the amount of pressure you are using if necessary.

Remember that the Weather Report is a gift that you are giving to another person.

This loving gift will be returned to you soon.

Change places with your partner and repeat the activity.

And at the end, if you enjoyed the Weather Report, be sure to thank your Weatherman!

Once Over Lightly

Purpose: help another person to relax the whole body

Stand behind your partner and move your two index fingers down from the top of the neck to the base of the spine.

As you are doing this, your partner will exhale and relax into an easy forward bend from the waist.

Standing alongside your partner, tap gently up and down either side of the spinal column with your fingertips.

Stimulate the top of the shoulders with your fists and with the sides of your hands.

Tap the head with your fingers like raindrops.

Clap both your hands up and down from the shoulder to the fingertips.

Repeat the same movement on the other arm.

Clap both your hands up and down from the hip to the foot.

Repeat the same movement on the other leg.

Check to see that your partner is comfortable being tapped on the seat.

If so, tap gently on the sides of the hips and the bottom of the seat.

Move your two index fingers up from the base of the spine to the neck.

As you are doing this, your partner will inhale and lift very slowly back to an upright position.

Change places with your partner so you both have a turn.

Note: This activity may also be done in groups of three — with one person bending forward and the other two people working on both sides of the body at once.

Then change places and repeat the activity two more times.

This activity is designed to help another person relax and feel good.

Be sure to adjust the amount of pressure you use so that your partner is comfortable.

Leaders should be very aware of any children who might become too rough with each other,

Get Ready to Fly

Purpose: stretch and strengthen the shoulders and upper back

Pretend that you are a dragon getting ready to fly to a magical place.

You need to strengthen your wings in preparation for your trip.

With a partner decide who is Dragon #1 and who is Dragon #2.

#1   Sit on the floor in a comfortable cross-legged position

#2   Stand facing your partner's back.

#1   Clasp your hands together behind your head and bring your elbows forward.

#2   Lean over your partner and place your hands on the outside of the elbows.

#1   Press your elbows away from each other.

#2   Press your partner's elbows toward each other.

      You are offering resistance to your partner in order to stretch the muscles on the outside of the arms.

Breathe in together for a few moments.

Then release your hands and your breath.

#1   With your hands still behind your head, spread your elbows apart and stretch your chest forward.

#2   Place your hands on the inside of your partner's elbows and help stretch the arms back.

Place one knee between the shoulder blades for support.

Be sure to ask your partner how that feels.

Pull back very gently only as far as your partner wants you to.

Then release your hands.

Exchange places with your partner and repeat the activity.

Now flap your wings and be ready to fly!

Dragons Really Are Alive

Purpose: help another person's shoulders feel good while having fun together.

Sit on the floor facing your partner's back.

Place your hands gently on the shoulders of the person in front of you.

Say the following words as you move your hands:

1 - 2 - 3 - 4
Dragons walking out the door

> Tap your palms slowly on your partner's shoulders in time with the rhythm of the words.

5 - 6 - 7 - 8
Dragons running through the gate

> Tap your palms a little faster.

8 - 7 - 6 - 5
Dragons really are alive!

> Tap your fingers very fast up and down your partner's arms and onto the head — like dragons running all around.

4 - 3 - 2 - 1
Dragons sleeping in the sun

> Place your hands gently on your partner's shoulders, helping them relax.

Exchange places with your partner and repeat the activity.

Note: This activity can be done with one person sitting in a chair and the other person standing. It can also be done with one person lying face down and the other person kneeling.

This activity usually produces lots of laughter on the third line. It is a safe and loving way for people to enjoy sharing physical touch.

Ten Little Dragons

Purpose: help another person feel energized and relaxed

Sit on the floor facing your partner's back.

Place your hands gently on the shoulders of the person in front of you and say the following words as you move your hands:

Ten little dragons sleeping in their bed

   (rest your hands on your partner's shoulders)

All climbed up to the top of the head

   (move your fingers up to the head)

Started dancing in the air

   (bounce your fingers around)

Running here and running there

   (move your fingers up and down the shoulders and arms)

They rolled down to the bottom of the hill
Then climbed up like Jack and Jill

   (move your fists down the back and up again)

Flying here and flying there
Dragons, dragons everywhere

   (move your hands all around in wide sweeping circles)

"Let's slow down," the dragons said

   (tap your palms slowly on the shoulders)

So ten little dragons went back to bed

   (rest your hands quietly and imagine sending warm energy into the muscles of your partner's back)

Poems and Songs

The Dragon and the Butterfly

There was a young dragon who lived in a cave,
His body was strong and his spirit was brave.
He roamed through the forests and munched on the trees,
He rode over rainbows and dove in the seas.
He circled the earth on incredible flights,
Looking for wild and magnificent sights.
His view of the world was extensive and wide,
His journey in life — an adventurous ride!

And there was a butterfly, gentle and small
Who lived in a garden inside of a wall.
She drank from the roses, she sang to the trees,
She floated on sunbeams and bounced on the breeze,
Her beauty was awesome, a joy to behold,
Her wings were of orange with splashes of gold.
The world that she knew was surrounded with green,
Her journey in life was relaxed and serene.

And how, you may ask, did these two ever meet?
Well listen, I'll tell you a story quite sweet.

The dragon loved flying around, as you know.
One morning he happened to notice below
A garden of roses all covered with dew,
And so he decided to try something new.
He flew to the ground and sat quietly there,
Smelling the blossoms and breathing the air,
Letting the stillness around him prevail
When all of a sudden he felt on his tail
A slight little tickle — he opened his eyes
And there he discovered a lovely surprise.

The tiniest creature that he'd ever seen
Was smiling at him with a spirit serene.

"Good morning, I'm happy to welcome you, sir.
I had no idea how gigantic you were."
The dragon said kindly, "Come rest on my wing,
I never have met such a delicate thing."

Soon they were talking and sharing their news,
Telling their stories, comparing their views.
The dragon whose world was so open and wide
Learned to be peaceful and venture inside.
The butterfly's world, so restricted and small,
Soon was expanded outside of her wall.

The dragon would place her inside of his ear,
Safe in a place where he knew she'd be near.
They rode over rainbows to lands far away,
And then they'd return to their garden each day,
Feeling a beautiful balance begin
Of joy on the outside and peace from within.

The Dragon's Hat

I'm sure you have heard of the Cat in the Hat.
One cold, cold, wet day he stepped in on the mat.
He said, "I will teach you some games that are new.
Here are my helpers, Thing One and Thing Two."

Well, I have a hat and a story to tell
And I have a dragon adventure, as well.
One day I was sitting out under a cloud,
Looking around me and thinking out loud.

"Our Earth is in trouble, that's something we know.
There's lots of pollution wherever we go.
Some people are selfish and don't seem to care.
We chop down the forests and stink up the air.
We're killing the wildlife, destroying the trees,
There's junk in the rivers and slime in the seas."

Then all of a sudden a dragon appeared
Wearing a hat and a long furry beard.
He sat very still and he watched me a while,
And then he came closer and said, with a smile,
"When I have a problem that troubles my dreams,
I put on my hat which is magic, it seems.
I sit very still and I listen inside
And trust what I hear from my wise inner guide.
My brain and my heart work together, it's true,
To help me decide on the best thing to do."

All creatures on earth are responsible for
Doing their part — and a little bit more.
So put on this hat and perhaps you will hear
Important reminders and messages clear.

Perhaps you'd be willing to tell us your dreams,
Creative ideas or original schemes.
What can you do that has value and worth
To help us improve how we live on this earth?

Note: Have a "magic hat" available to place on the
head of anyone in the group who wishes to share some
ideas.

Let Your Dragons Rest

Tune: Go Down Moses

When you've got too much to do
    Give your brain a rest
Relaxation helps you to
    Give your brain a rest
Slow down, dragons,
Then you'll be at your best
Take a breath and tell yourself to
    Give your brain a rest

When there is a lot to see
    Give your eyes a rest
Look inside and quietly
    Give your eyes a rest
Slow down, dragons,
Then you'll be at your best
Take a breath and tell yourself to
    Give your eyes a rest.

When you have a lot to say
    Give your voice a rest
Silently throughout the day
    Give your voice a rest
Slow down, dragons,
Then you'll be at your best
Take a breath and tell yourself to
    Give your voice a rest.

When you start to feel upset
    Give your heart a rest
There's no need to fuss and fret
    Give your heart a rest
Slow down, dragons,
Then you'll be at your best
Take a breath and tell yourself to
    Give your heart a rest.

When you're feeling tense and tight
    Give your back a rest
You'll sleep better through the night
    Give your back a rest
Slow down, dragons,
Then you'll be at your best
Take a breath and tell yourself to
    Give your back a rest.

When you want to be at peace
    Give yourself a rest
Let your cares and worries cease
    Give yourself a rest
Slow down, dragons,
Then you'll be at your best
Take a breath and tell yourself to
    Give yourself a rest.

Find some quiet time each day to
    Let your dragons rest
As your troubles float away
    Let your dragons rest
Slow down, dragons,
Then you'll be at your best
Take a breath and tell yourself to
    Let your dragons rest.

The Dragon Dream

Polly and her puppy dog
Went out to take a walk
Along the stream she had a dream
And she began to talk.

"Puppy, you're my dearest friend
I love you best of all
You're full of fun, you like to run
And follow when I call.

I had a dream this morning
I'd like to cast a spell
So you can change to something strange
And magical as well."

Polly tripped upon a log
And stumbled to the ground
When she stood up, her little pup
Was nowhere to be found.

Instead she saw a dragon
She looked into his eyes
They said "Hello," she felt his glow
And knew that he was wise.

They walked along the river
And ran around the bend
"Come ride and play with me today
And be my special friend."

Poly climbed upon his back
And held a silver cord
Away they flew into the blue
And then they really soared!

Polly told her dragon friend
A dream she had to share
That war would cease and seeds of peace
Would flower everywhere.

"You can help to make it true"
The little dragon said,
"The place to start is in your heart
And right inside your head.

Look within and ask yourself
What peace is really worth
And then just start to do your part
To build a better earth."

"But I am just a little girl
The world's so big," said she,
"It doesn't seem as though my dream
Could ever come to be."

"Each dream is very magical
You know that this is so
And when you care, the love you share
Around the world will go.

A billion other children
Are dreamers just like you
I wonder whether all together
You can make it true."

Polly and her dragon friend
Both thought about the dream
And when it ended, they descended
Back beside the stream

And then the dragon disappeared
As if by magic charms
When she stood up, her little pup
Was snuggled in her arms.

"I have so much to tell you!"
She looked into his eyes
And then she knew her puppy too
Was magical and wise.

They hugged and kissed each other
They knew that it was so
That when we care, the love we share
Around the world will go.

A billion other people
Are dreamers just like YOU
I wonder whether all together
WE can make it true!

Am I Singing the Song That I Came Here to Sing?

Am I singing the song that I came here to sing?
Am I bringing to earth all the joy I can bring?
Am I dancing to music composed from above,
Vibrations of harmony, beauty and love?

Am I keeping my life in a natural key
So that I may become what I came here to be?
As I think, so I am; as I'm living I find
That my life has a tempo in tune with my mind.

Am I feeling those rhythms within and afar,
Directing my heartbeat — or guiding a star?
Am I hearing the symphony Nature plays
Composed in eternal and infinite ways?

Am I chanting the song that accompanies birth
Of the wonder and joy of existence on earth!

Inner Knowing

I close my eyes, allow my sight
To focus on my Inner Light
I look within for clarity
And through the darkness I can see.

I listen, listen deep inside
To wisdom from my Inner Guide
I listen for a message clear
And in the silence I can hear.

I still my breath and feel the flow
Of silent self with Inner Glow
Within the stillness love can heal
And in that knowing peace is real.

Pray for Peace

In the moments of the morn
when the day is being born

> Pray for peace

When you're standing at the sink
with some moments free to think

> Pray for peace

When you're putting on your shoes
and you hear the daily news

> Pray for peace

When you dance and sing and play
let the song within you say

> Pray for peace

When you're watching children run
laughing freely in the sun

> Pray for peace

When you're starting up your car
take a moment where you are to

> Pray for peace

When you're entering the door
of an office or a store

> Pray for peace

When the checkout line is long
keep your peaceful vision strong

> Pray for peace

When your call is put on HOLD
let your thoughts of peace unfold

> Pray for peace

When the traffic line is slow
breathe in peace and feel it flow

Pray for peace

When you're sitting by the fire
and the flames are leaping higher

Pray for peace

At the ending of the day
when you meditate and pray

Pray for peace

CPSIA information can be obtained at www.ICGtesting.com

262129BV00001B/4/A